Untranslatable

T0099253

Untranslatable
Kääntää
Intraducibile
Intraduisible
Lefordíthatatlan
Uobersættelig
Onvertaalbaar
Nepřeložitelné
סוגריתל ןתינ אל
Nieprzetumaczalne
Intraduzível
Непереводимые

Poems by
Julia Klatt Singer

NORTH STAR PRESS OF ST. CLOUD, INC.
St. Cloud, Minnesota

to spring

Cover image © iStock/Getty Images

Copyright © 2015 Julia Klatt Singer

ISBN: 978-0-87839-789-1

First edition: March 1, 2015

Printed in the United States of America

Published by
North Star Press of St. Cloud, Inc.
P.O. Box 451
St. Cloud, MN 56302

www.northstarpress.com

Table of Contents

Ayurnamat

(Inuktitut) The philosophy that there is no reason to worry about the things that can't be changed.

When you appear in my dream
talking, as if I'd been there all along
I hand you a knife, don't even have to ask
if you'd like to help. We are twenty-five stories;
from the ground, into the evening,
making dinners, watching the snow.
Always with you there is falling
snow, from a window that reminds me
of a bed, there, where your eyes rest,
there, where I dream,
as the snow swirls and spells out
all the things we've left
unsaid.

Snjór

(Icelandic) One of the 6,243 words identified to name the snow or its appearance.

The silence of snow,
like the silence of you
is what I wake to

blinding white
and falling.
Start the day

By throwing away
words;
scarlet, indigo, then

cerulean, mango
who needs them
in this kind of cold?

Take apart my name
letter by letter
toss each one to the crows.

Bury me in white,
bury me away
like your heart.

What animal owns it now?
What kind of spring
will it take

to trigger your blood
to run
honey & sweet.

Waldeinsamkeit

(German) The feeling of being alone in the woods.

First, I must tune out the opera
my husband is listening to on the radio, now
the applause—it sounds genuine,
but from this distance (both geographical and of time)
there is something hollow, something less than
true as it thunders in our living room.
Tonight I don't need the German
or the tenor or the tiptoeing violins.
Or the clicking nails of our dog
as he walks from room to room in search
of a register that is warm, to claim and own.
Then there is the wind that twists
the porch chimes into a frenzied song. Ahab
too, who spent most of his years
watching the Sound from my in-laws' verandah
now fights the Canadian cold fronts,
his wooden back clattering against the house.
It is the right kind of darkness, moonless
like walking under trees thick with canopy.
I imagine the woods, and how I'd walk through them
but the soprano is still singing
just hit her high note—
I may be alone in my wishing her quiet
but I wish it anyway. Put her in a real woods
night trees, charcoal silhouettes
drawn against an inky sky.
They band together
a chorus of trees, hush
the wind (the soprano too)
let winter still and cold
settle in. In deepest winter
let me walk,
a small lit thing,
ever so quietly through
the tracks of something else's making.

Yugen

(Japanese) An awareness of the universe that triggers emotional responses too deep and mysterious to be described.

I set the oven to self-cleaning
so that I can at least smell heat.
Minus fourteen outside, the house wears
the chill of winter, in its fabric
and in its seams.

I am no different,
Winter is my bones;
my thoughts are frost
my breath, a cloud
my heart, a buried sun.

Culaccino

(Italian) The mark left on a table by a cold glass.

The first one I remember
was lemonade, on the kitchen counter
then strawberries in the colander,
sun in the water from the tap
that washed over them. I fell in love
with water—preferred it over anything else—
drank it down, cold and clear
filled my belly till I could feel it through my skin.

The next was whisky, on the card table
the click of ice, the laughter of men—
deep and knowing. My parents
and their best friends from college
played a game, *I Never*
that my mother almost always won
because, as she said, *sometimes*
not doing something is worth more
than having done it.
I remember running my finger
around the watermarks
their glasses made, I remember
thinking how perfect each circle was
and how all it took was a drink
to make it.

Iktsuarpok

(Inuit) The feeling of anticipation that leads you to keep looking outside to see if anyone is coming.

The snow is pale and blue, the sky
the soft pink of a girl's palm.
The dog tries to shake the cold
from his fur, as both of us stand
here at the window, watching
for that something; bird
wind, fox, early bear, anything
really, that like us is
flesh hungry, heart beating
steady.

Komorebi

(Japanese) Sunlight that filters through the leaves of trees.

In winter
we forget
how the sun feels
upon skin
how it sinks in
deep, so deep
even our blood, even our bones
can feel how it sleeps
upon the leaves
lingers away
sweet afternoons—
like you do, on your back
naming the clouds,
(later your skin smells
like grass)
like I do, remembering.
Both of us knowing
a warm wind
is all we need
to shake beauty
free.

Vedriti

(Slovenian) To take shelter from the rain.

We live longer than a hummingbird
    but not as long as an elm

are nothing compared to the wind
    but like the rain, are forecasted

will fall, will come again and
    even though I've told you

to take your umbrella, you
    forget. Just as I forget

how the world is made new
    by each rain, with each kiss.

Astre

(French) "Celestial body," anything that shines in the night sky.

Leave the gate open
for the moon.

Your heart, like a star,
leads you home.

Lying in bed, you feel its heat
trapped beneath your ribs.

Mokita

(New Guinean) The truth everyone knows but nobody says.

We need the skin of another sometimes
to feel our own.

We need crows to gather
Land on every branch of every tree

to remind us
We are not alone.

A drink helps
Music, more so.

Winter is a continent; bodies hibernate
thoughts migrate.

Need the sun on our backs, to reach the soil.
Need mud, melting snow.

Need the earth to open herself up.
Need ants to cross the hills of our shins.

We need to feel
lucky again.

Lagom

(Swedish) Just at a right amount, "lagom lång" (the right height) or "lagom varmt" (the optimal heat).

No more talk about the weather
No more pretending
It is going to get any better
Than this
and about happiness
Take me dancing
and I will show you
What happiness
looks like, until you too
Can feel it
in the swing and in the beat
in each chord, and at your feet
in your body, easy as air
in the gentle give
and there
in your wrists, and
your hips, a blown kiss,
at your fingertips.

Torschlusspanik

(German) "Gate-closing panic," the fear of diminishing opportunities as one ages.

Wish I was
out stealing horses
taking down fences
following the sun—
or maybe my heart—

most likely the scent
of creosote and tallgrass
mostly likely your ghosts
come and go when there's music,
when there's wind.

Who needs a body
when there's no one
to dance with. Who needs
hands when you've got nothing
to hold.

S'entendre

(French) "Hearing each other," get along with someone,
understand how they think.

You believe love to be something pure and clean when it isn't.
Certain moments, you will live them, as long as you're living.
There is no escape. Like the heat of him. What it means
to be drawn in. There is no word, no name for this, except his.
It's all whisky, the shine of the bar, mirrors, smoke. He carries
the scent of the sun on his skin, the weather in his lapels.
The light is cold, for February. The sun is clean and bright
and not much else. Sometimes busted love is love enough.

Retrouvailles

*(French) The feeling of happiness on meeting someone again
who you haven't seen for a very long time.*

At the heart of it,
it has always been you.
Your long lean gaze
Your sleep-with-me eyes
The way you slip
Your voice into her hair
Tangle it, with the everydayness
She breaths in of you, lets you
Travel through
all the places you have been,
all the places she wants to go too.
She pictures now the postcard you'll send
when you get there.

Kaapshljmurslis

(Latvian) The feeling of being cramped while riding public transportation during rush hour.

I learned how to side-stroke, crawl
dead man float and surface dive
in the June cold water of Silver Lake.
Silver Lake's water nowhere near silver, so green-gray-blue
the sun couldn't find its way through.
Swimming underwater, I wondered if this is what it felt like
to be blind. I was a body
moving, feeling my way with my hands and
thighs—god the weeds how they startled me
reached for my skin.
I remember the panic,
losing my direction, seeing only the shadows
of weeds, nothing familiar, no trees, no sky.
I remember my lungs, panging for air.
Years later, as a mother, riding the Paris metro
at rush hour with my two-year-old, six months pregnant
with my second son, crowded in a car
with barely room to stand, it was this feeling, of being underwater
this feeling of airlessness, of near panic that returned.
Thoughts do not help, thinking.
It is your body that saves you. It is desire.
For the earth, for the air, for solid ground
for someone's hand to find, to hold.

Duende

(Spanish) The mysterious power a work of art has to deeply move a person.

The sky
looks like it is fire
the lake, silver
and I wonder
what my skin tastes like
after seeing something
like this.
For surely
this sky falls, sinks
beneath my skin
just as the cold does, just
as the snow. Just as the moon
does, when it is waning,
just as the clouds do
when they can't help but break.
Some moments I am nothing more
than driftwood, fox prints, flight.

Saudade

*(Portuguese) The feeling of longing for something or some-
one whom you love and which is lost.*

If I had to give him a season, a weather,
he'd be fall, the harvest moon, the tractor,
the way its light travels the field, its trailing veil of dust.

The crunch of gravel, of twigs, of bones.
He'd be the thicket
the grouse hides in, the scent of burning

leaves, the shroud of night, the path
smoke takes, the way a voice can lead you
closer than you've ever been.

Every kind of gray; dove and ash
charcoal and cement, spiderweb,
dust, old bruise, held breath.

He was the kind of hour
you lose, the kind of day
you can't forget.

Jaksaa

(Finnish) The lack of energy to do something, just too tired.

If there is beauty
it must be found
in ice
in the absence
of color, of life
in the piety
of cold
of air taken
and collapsed
in half
and in half again.
Bodies buried
under fibers
and skins
until we cannot recognize
our own.
Why bother?
Even the birds
have quit
their routines.
Three jays
squat at the feeder.
One rabbit
cuts the yard
into triangles.
Cold isn't round
but all straight lines
blue and barbed,
an arrow that pierces
my skin, my heart,
each thought,
to the bone.

тьмутаракань

*(Russian) The back of beyond, the middle of nowhere, the
underdeveloped depths of the country.*

I am not quite there, the middle of nowhere
because I can see from my window
the lights of a freight train—
three, stacked, like the plastic triangle
you put around the pool balls—it must have a name,
that thing, but it is lost to me now—
even though I remember the way the light fell
in swatches, how the balls held no heat,
the certainty of the pool cue
in my hands, the soft hush
of the table, and that as the balls broke
I thought first of the big bang (planetary)
then sex (now the rumbling of the train).
As I wait for you (orbiting)
to come into view.

Knygnešys

(Lithuanian) "Book carrier." When the Russian Tsar restricted the press, Knygnešiai saved the Lithuanian language and culture by transporting illegal books printed in Prussia.

In Miina's garden grew
the offspring from her mother's garden
in Virrat, Finland.
Before Miina set sail for America,
her mother carefully sewed seeds
and roots into the hem
of her skirt. Miina hoped
that no one would notice
the little bundles, the earthy smell—
more out of embarrassment
than the guilt of smuggling.

As she grew old, each flower
and vegetable became prayers
to a world she'd never see again.

Once she saw the face of her baby brother
in a pansy, her father's nose in a zucchini.
What flower would she be, she wondered
and who would remember her?

Tɒāj

(Thai) Sincere kindness and willingness to help others, even before they asked, without expecting something in return.

We can't put back what time releases.
We can't walk through this city built of bricks
of glass, of steel, and not flinch, not want
our fathers in their heavy black work shoes and
boots holding our hands, their nails clipped
and clean, the only trace of despair
in sinewy arms and a thirst
we do not understand and
cannot quench.

Yaourter

(French) "Chanter en yaourt/yaourter"—Literally "to yoghurt," this expression is used for someone trying to sing in a foreign language and getting the words wrong.

When Max was four, he told me that he knew what a tomato was.
It's a big wind that can blow down your house.

That's a tornado, honey, I said, *Not a tomato.*

Oh, his brow furrowed, *Well I'm watching for tomatoes in the sky,*
      just in case.
I wouldn't want one to hit you, Mommy, or the house. It would
      make a mess.

I smile, tell him, *I'll take your advice*
      and watch for tomatoes too.

I'd like all my troubles to take shape, to be tomatoes.
Ripe and drooping from the vine, I'd know when

the stem was going to give, when the skin
was going to shatter, the seeds, scatter.

Or mangos, they're a lovely color, mango.
I'd see them coming for sure.

Coconuts, so heavy and solid, a satisfying crack.
Trouble should have such a sound.

Voorpret

*(Dutch) "Pre-fun," the sense of enjoyment one can feel
before an event actually takes place.*

It is just me and two Somali women
running the track tonight.
It is February, a Saturday night,
and I am sick of snow, of ice, of cold.
Sick of being careful, of watching
my step. Sick of being buried
under layers and layers of clothing. I fantasize
about the hour that it is warm enough to not need
boots, hat, mittens, scarf, socks, jacket
and how I'll take them off, leave them
in a pile on the road, just walk away
like I'd like to walk away
from winter. I am running tonight
just to make sure I'll be ready
to dash—all arms and legs
and lungs into spring. It is then
that I notice the head scarf
of the woman running in front of me
how it swings behind her
as if it is waving hello.

Yuputka

(Ulwa) The feeling you get when, walking in the forest, you imagine that someone (or something) touches your skin.

The spring after my father died
I'd slip into his closet, shyly
close the door, stand
in the semi-darkness—
always there was a slim shaft of light
between the door and the floor
between the door and its frame.
I'd let my eyes adjust,
my head rest against the shoulder
of one of his shirts, skeletal
on the wire hanger, as my hands
found the cuff. Nose buried
in the cotton I'd breathe in
what was left of the scent
of him.
Remembering
when he was still alive,
only weeks ago, how I'd stand
my body thin and flat
against the wall behind the front door
so that when he came home
he wouldn't see me,
wouldn't know where I was.
How'd I'd wait
for him to find me—
knew he'd always find me—
brush his whiskers
against my cheek, place
a kiss on my forehead,
my favorite hello.

Pälvi

(Finnish) A "bald" place in the snow in the spring, when the snow begins to melt.

I want a new word
for *longing*

something that evokes the lull, the lustrous
hankering, the narrow spare urgency of it.

We both know how
it can roam and ramble, tilt to luck

but I'm talking about *a longing* tinged and
ravaged, lain by appetite.

A *word* that could even make
this polished steel of a sky blush.

The kind of word that slips down a hallway
but not unnoticed

passes through you
like light does a door, when it is left ajar

and lays itself down, lingers
until it sweetens the honey wood of the floor.

Madrugar

(Spanish) To get up before sunrise or get up earlier than usual.

(When the rest of the world wasn't paying any attention)
All the birds went the way of the sun
All the trees swayed
All the clouds broke down to one
All the colors found their edges
Let their seams fray.

Heard the rain say
fall silver, linger.
Heard my heart say
Stay, please, stay
even though
I knew
you were going
always going
were already on
your way.

Sisu

(Finnish) "To have guts."

Leave me the rafters
take away the roof

our fortune can be found
in the distance between stars

in the space to roam, space
to get lost, just

Leave me the inky blue
dusk paints on you, your

explorer eyes
and this winter sky

and a hundred crows
how they leaf winter trees

until their king says fly—
they fill the sky

an airborne alphabet
words form

take the shape of clouds
then fall, soft and white.

Take away the roof
leave me the rafters

lie down by my side
let night find

our resilience; all our hard letters,
all our soft sounds.

Luftmensch

(Yiddish) Social misfit, an impractical dreamer with no business sense. Literally, "air person."

I could live on air
Not this stale February
after-dinner in-the-house air, but the air
just after it rains, even the air
after it snows

if the wind is still and the moon is kind.
And the air, that carries
the scent of a wood-burning fire
that I can live on for a week,
maybe more.

Or the air, the wind,
that longs for the wings
of the birds
that haven't yet
returned.

Ukiyo

*(Japanese) The "floating world," a place of fleeting beauty
and living in the moment, detached from the bothers of life.*

Always at the edge
of something beautiful; an ocean, a day, a cliff,
a field, a bed.

Sky is a must, blue or bruised
with clouds, I don't care
just the endlessness of it.

I am a bird, fleeting as my song.
I am an animal, nothing more
than hunger, skin, heart, bones.

You are a must,
blue or bruised by clouds,
I don't care. You are the ocean, each day,

each edge,
the field I want to lie down in, make of it
a sweet bed.

Gökotta

*(Swedish) To wake up early in the morning with the purpose
of going outside to hear the first birds sing.*

Somewhere, between the pines and the lake the sun breaks through,
branch by branch.

It takes its time
to get to me, just as it takes its time

to warm the path, rust-colored pine needles
bathed in sun, their scent rises.

I never needed words
when I was with you, just a bird calling, another, taking flight.

Just to be held in your gaze, for a moment
just to be held like the sun.

Geländesprung

(German) Lightly skipping over the surface of something.

I follow my shadow
out to the edge
of the ice cliff
watch it dive
into the water.
Later the moon
will leave a slim path
of stardust and ash
just long enough
to reach you.

Mamihlapiatapai

(Yagán, originally Yahgan) The look of understanding people exchange when they realize they are of the same opinion.

The snow casts blue shadows
as if the sky too
has given up.
It lies in each hollow,
upon each windswept grave.

I haven't seen a bird in days.
Just the fox, on the beach
who runs when he sees me
to the lake ice—miles and miles of it—
heads east towards the sun.

Boketto

*(Japanese) The act of gazing vacantly into the distance
without thinking.*

I wake to nouns;
Window, rafters, snow, roof,
ash, cement, dawn.
Adjectives shake loose from
icicles, slender and piercing.
Trees frame the eastern sky
and somewhere out there
is you,
what you are
waking to.

Uitwaaien

*(Dutch) To take a walk and get some fresh air. Also
translated as to walk in the wind for fun.*

He tells me all he wants to do is drink and
Listen to Leonard Cohen. I picture a Hopper scene,
brick apartment, a thin-curtained
window, a man with a drink,
down to the ice
he holds in both hands. He is lit
by a solitary light.
Night has fallen indigo
and smoke, and the wind
smells like coming rain.
I am walking
the same night, but in
a different city, walking
dark, quiet streets
my feet moving
to the beat
of someone else's song.

Panapo'o

*(Hawaiian) The act of scratching your head in order to help
you remember something you have forgotten.*

We forget about the things we've forgotten—the jack-o-lanterns
and rake, the broken end of the shovel, the dead bat—
all emerge as the snow recedes.
Spring isn't just about new life, about purity
but about exposing us
for who we are, for what we've done.
Old tennis balls and sleds and the husks of sunflower seeds
say we tried to live outside ourselves.
Mid-March and I am like this quarter, shimmering
in the sunlight, still frozen under a layer of ice.

Moit

*(Scottish) Pretended indifference/shyness while speaking
about a thing one is very keen for.*

You tell me to keep my hands open
palms facing up
Tell me I can leave this world
with my breath, can learn to meditate.
I wonder
how my body can contain me.
The distance between
letters, these letters,
is further than I feel from you.
But I stick to the format
Stay out of the margins
Do not take too much space
Even though
I'd like to fill in each blank, fill the whole of your space,
like rainclouds fill the sky, like darkness surrounds each star,
like the crows fill each branch of each bare February tree,
and I'd write this poem on your body let the words spill and
mingle from your elbow
to your floating rib
Leave a *kiss*
on your wrist
Leave a *comma*
on each
finger
tip.

Itadakimasu

(Japanese) A phrase to start a meal with gratitude to all:
from cooks and farmers to lives to be eaten.

We've just left the Alps.
The fields are dotted with crimson,
poppies the train rushes through—
waifish stems, wild and paper-thin—
I unbutton my shirt
Let the sun find my skin.

Later we walk through
the market. Feathered birds
hang by their feet, dirt thin dogs
lie in the shade of trucks, of crates.
I smell fresh blood, smell ripe tomatoes too,
the bitter leaves, the sun in them.

Every hunger
starts with a sound, becomes a word.
Every desire takes a physical form.
I ask you to step a little closer
I need to smell, need to feel
the earth the sky the rain
in you.

Nakkele

(Tulu) A man who licks whatever the food has been served on.

Breakfast is your dream
retold, in Technicolor
when you get to the part
where you don't know
which city you're in
or where you are running to, from
I wrap my legs around yours,
recite your address,
write your zip code
on your chest
with my fingertip.

Lunch is a picnic.
I am both plate and table
napkin and the wine you spill
red ripe fruit
seeds, skin in your teeth.

Dinner is dusk, an indigo sky.
We wait for the moonlight
to angle from the table,
find the floor.
I am a cricket and you
the first star.
We are nightfall—
stirring branches,
hushed light.

Donaldkacsázás

(Hungarian) Literally "Donald Ducking," this word describes
the practice of wearing a shirt but no trousers at home.

And what's the word for never taking your socks off?
Whether it is laziness or climate related?
Would we differentiate?
And how about the feeling of dread when one puts on last summer's
swimsuit? There has to be a word for that.
Hand-me-downs—almost one word,
but what about the feeling we have for those jeans/shirts/sweaters
we've got pictures of our brothers/sisters/cousins wearing?
I loved wearing my friends' clothes in college.
Loved trading shirts and jeans.
It was almost as good as sex, feeling the fabric
of someone else's shirt against my skin,
breathing in the scent of them.
Barbie Heels—now that's a condition
and paper dolling (always wearing the proper underwear
and having good posture, square shoulders
so your clothes don't fall off).
Duluth has got its share of Santas—bearded men
who favor red. I just hope they aren't Donald Ducking
and if they are,
please, please, no red-and-white furry-topped socks.

Fensterln

(German) Climbing through a window to avoid someone's parents in order to have sex with the someone without the parents knowing.

The moon tonight
is a cracked egg,
the sky, spilled ink.
I am a wisp of a cloud,
and you
the tree, the elm
majestic and arching
I see from my window.
I want nothing more
than to be tangled
in your branches,
blanketed in starlight.

Goya

(Urdu) The transporting suspension of disbelief that can occur; good storytelling.

He is a word, a strong and kind one, a verb
And a noun. She finds him each night

at dusk, traces the path he leaves for her
from her backdoor into the garden.

Tonight he smells of dirt and peonies.
She picks up a petal, shaped like the moon

presses it to her palm. Other words now
become him. He is the letter *s*, a small *x*.

He is the hollow of her belly, where her jeans
hit the bone of her hip. He is the ink on her fingers,

the first day warm enough to go without shoes.
Some nights he is the rustling of leaves

others, the first planet she sees.
Tonight he is the sound of crickets, proof.

Badkruka

*(Swedish) Someone who is reluctant to get into the water
when swimming outdoors.*

My father taught me how to swim,
taught me the way he knew how, said to me
You are gonna sink.
Or you are gonna swim.
He held me in his arms, I was three, maybe four.
One or the other, he shrugged his shoulders.
My mom sat in the shade of an old towering oak tree—
she looked like a girl
there at its base. She was lost in a book,
had it open in her lap,
her legs curled under her like a doe.
She never swam with us at the lake.
It took coaxing to get her to walk to the edge
of it, stick her toes in.
She didn't like to be wet.
She didn't like the sun.
She was a redhead, had skin like the underbelly of fish—
that's what she said.
What are you going to do? He asked me,
Ready? Set?
Sink. I said.
Go! He released me, into the water.
I felt my body sink, become a rock,
felt the cool of the water.
Eyes open, I saw the sun's rays angling
through it. Felt my body rise
to the surface. Feet and hands pushing
against water.
My dad, hands and elbows and arms and chest and shoulders
in front of me, smiling, saying
No, swim.

42

Oka

*(Ndunda) Difficulty urinating due to eating too many frogs
when the rainy season hasn't started yet.*

I wrote twenty things and erased them all
1. What I remember about losing my virginity is how the moon
2. was there, in the room too and after, how quiet the world was
3. like fishing with my grandfather,
4. learning the way of water, of reeds, living in a steel blue world
5. loving like rain, like thunder.
6. Why do all my memories come down to this;
7. the scent of peonies, a radio in the background,
8. the light through a window that feels like a blessing.
9. Birds come to mind and crickets, the nights of fireflies—
10. their beauty makes me weep.
11. To let love guide you
12. to let the darkness envelop you
13. to shine
14. to fail to shine
15. to carry on
16. to carry on.
17. And to find the lake, with a skim of ice so thin
18. it can only hold the moon
19. like a glance,
20. like a brush of a hand.

Orka

(Swedish) To not have the ability or energy to be able to do something any longer.

Today there is only the remnants
of love
left under your skin.
You can't swap blood
for wine
although you'd like to try.
When it comes right down to it
we can
live off so little—
a bud of hope, a berry.
Tomorrow, you tell me,
there will be fruit,
juicy and red.

Ládramhaíola

(Irish, Gaelic) A wasted day, although it was intended to be a productive one.

It's a small thing, to take an *s*, make it an *ed*.
From present to past only requires stealing five
small letters—vowels, soft sounds.
We are growing accustomed to this;
the wasted hours,
the sin without letting it sink
in. After,
we find a small *k*
on the kitchen floor—
mistake it
for a broken wing
of a butterfly.

Sobremesa

*(Spanish) The time spent, after lunch or dinner, talking to
the people you shared the meal with.*

The table, set with the sun.
The peonies blush, her eyes, laugh—
for her, it is enough—
to eat a meal is to eat the world.

The silver lined up in a row
glasses glasses plates and forks,
now that the sky is indigo, have found their way back
to the kitchen, are done

for the night. She is telling
the story about Bill's wedding and the dashikis.
No one cares that she's told it before.
Another bottle of wine is opened,

another napkin hits the floor.
The windows are glossy black,
reflect all of us, the table, the room.
The moon is the first to leave.

Zhaghzhagh

(Persian) The chattering of teeth from the cold or from rage.

A hawk
chased by a crow
zigzags through the branches
flying low,
swoops and lands
in the tree
outside my window, feathers ruffled
he shakes it off.
The crow circles above, glossy black
against a pale gray sky.
I envy their flight,
their physicality, whole body
in chase in motion in retreat.
It doesn't matter who is right
who's been wronged,
the sun finds their wings
just the same.

Mångata

(Swedish) The road-like reflection of the moon on the water.

You hold the moon in your hands,
peel it, place a slice on my tongue.

Ask me not to speak,
to feel instead, tell me

everything catches light, catches fire
when it has the room to breathe.

I want to give you this night
this unnamable sea we stand at the edge of

my thoughts
small ripples at the shore,
your body

the path the moon takes.

Koyaanisqatsi

(Hopi) Nature out of balance.

Have you forgotten how darkness tucks itself in
as the stars, one by one, say hello?

The call of a bird, you know by heart,
follows you home.

Even if we could turn back the clock
find ourselves in each song on the radio,

tune in, volume low.
Even if I could find you,

a thin long-legged boy, hiding
in the fort in the empty lot on my childhood street

I'd still ask you to look at the sky.
Name for me the color it is now.

Toska

(Russian) a dull ache of the soul.

You might mistake sunlight for optimism
(you might be right too).
We do not need to suffer
the long cold winter, we do not need the sensation
of having survived, in order to appreciate
the first warm afternoon,
one made of quiet clouds
unnamable blues.
You can tell something good
right off. Trust this,
but don't expect it to last any longer,
because you do.
It's okay to want. It's okay to ask
for things, to ask
questions too.
But not essential. Better
to live, to watch
the light break through
the tail end of a cloud.
Better to close your eyes
let the sun
find you.

Kairos

(Greek) The intuition of the moment.

Fact. At the stoplight I see you walking
across the sky on an invisible wire. Walking
towards the sun. You have your hands in your pockets,
showing me how easily it can be done.

Fact. The school bus, in front of me, standard
school bus yellow, is a Bluebird. That's what it says
on the white label below the door, the one
with the words *Emergency Exit* on it.

We are told
so many things, believe
when we can
that words, that facts, that truth will save us.

This moment I believe
that you are this bird, this small sooty one,
that flies low, swoops over my shoulder,
takes with it, my heart.

Shlimazl

(Yiddish) A chronically unlucky person.

Is most likely allergic to clover.
Bets on horses with names like
Tastes like Chicken, and Don't-Even-Think-About-It.
Is the son of a copper miner and a farmer.
Is probably Finnish. Has one of those names
you have to spell out, letter by letter
A-N-O, knowing its meaning,
Asked for,
will haunt him as much as knowing
he was child number eleven, and nobody was asking.
And that penny, in the road,
he is so tempted
to pick up (o copper, o how you glisten)
treasure and danger, how he wants
to pry it, from the tar,
free.

Togok

(Malay) To drink from a bottle in huge gulps.

One winter night in Minneapolis long ago

They want me to check my sled, don't even blink
that I have a sled, that I've brought it to the bar.
It is that kind of night and Moby Dick's is that kind of place.

After a day of swiftly falling snow, the city is quiet,
hushed into a sleep only winter can heap upon
all these countless avenues and streets.

I am young enough to still go sledding,
old enough to drink afterwards.
A glass of whisky sits on the bar. We choose

the stools next to it, order beer
unbutton our coats, unwind our scarves.
It is then the owner of the whisky returns.

He is wiry, wild-eyed and has a gauze bandage
wrapped around his head like a sweatband
I remember tennis players in the '70s wearing.

He sits downs, tents all ten of his fingers
on the glass. I turn to him, say hello.
He looks me in the eye, says

Head wound
then picks up his glass, holds it in the air.
You smell like snow, he says. *And happiness.*

Zwischenraum

(German) The space between things.

The nights your mother is in the next room dying
your younger brother and you sit up in the hospital lounge
late into the night drinking whisky, telling stories.
It is both vigil and voodoo. Something in you believes
that the stories will keep her and you and him alive.
Your brother hasn't heard most of them. He is
fourteen years younger than you, born after your father
had died. So you tell him about how at three
your dad was bribed with Fig Newtons
to get on the train with his aunt Auni, leave
Chicago for the U.P., the town his mother came from,
where he would spend the next three years
surrounded by cows and cousins, copper mines
and the kind of work that keeps one just
on the edge of poverty. And how your mother,
her high school class valedictorian, met him at Cartage
College, got pregnant with your brother Dan
and cobbled a family together. Your family.
It is superstition you have learned; do not talk
about pain, about hardship, about sin. Do not stop
working, do not sleep. Pray if you must.
Make your communion out of stories, out of whisky.
Press your tongue against the roof of your mouth,
like the needle of her IV drip, in her last good vein,
is pressed, with tape, to the back of her hand.

Nadi

(Balinese) To temporarily inhabit another dimension.

You slip in the door
carrying winter

on your back.
Unbutton your coat, let me

warm my hands with the music
in you.

Leave, like I knew you would, heading north.
Let the spool of thread unwind

until there is nothing
except the horizon, a bone thin moon, dirt

the promise
they hold.

Crouch in the ditch
redwings, blackbirds.

Become shadow,
take flight.

Aware

(Japanese) The bittersweetness of a brief and fading moment of transcendent beauty.

The street is a river of rain
swift and strong enough to carry
twigs and sticks, the occasional tumbling fallen petal.
Whitecaps form at the small rocks, sand
becomes a miniature beach. Last fall's leaves
now afloat, tiny spinning boats.
On the roof ten thousand raindrops.
Sometimes, an audience clapping.
Sometimes, stomping children's feet.
When they hush
the air in the room takes notice
holds its breath and waits
for the thunder
to roll to rumble.
My heart how it anticipates
beats out in Morse code,
my love, this love, for this
and every storm.

Wundersucht

(German) Passion for miracles.

We pretend each day
has a number, has a name
when in ours heart we know
there is only this
hour, this
sun now setting (the one that will rise
tomorrow, his older
brother) just as you
my darling can now hear
this first cricket spring
into summer. His legs
convey memory;
of longing, of dust
of ash & sparks,
tiny fires.

Won

(Korean) The reluctance to let go of an illusion.

There is something about water
when it leaves its banks
that makes me wonder why any of us
think our skin can contain us.

Hari kuyo

(Japanese) Shrine for broken sewing needles.

The kitchen drawer next to the sink was stuffed
full of used teabags. Another,
washed and worn Ziplock bags and old nylons.

Small torn pieces of paper
in her handwriting
are left like clues

in southern Baptist churches
people will say, loudly, Amen, after the preacher
has said something they agree with.

And
remember to tell Julia
about the tomatoes.

Behind the canned spinach and sauerkraut
you find the cookie tin full of buttons.
When you were little she let you play with them,

telling you the story
of where each had been
before its demise;

the tiny pearl one from your mother's first dress,
the wooden one from your grandfather's sweater,
the black velvet one from the dress she wore

to his funeral. To this day,
you can't help
but see in each one,

the hands that unbuttoned it
the history it clothed, how all that holds life in place
is a needle-thin thread.

59

Fernwah

(German) The opposite of homesickness (heimweh), feeling homesick for a place you have never been.

We hurl stones into the lake
watch them fracture the surface
turn the gray water
into silver beads of light.

We cannot see
if they twist and turn
or plummet
to the bed below.

How many years
did it take this stone
to form, to surface,
to break,

to smooth,
to be on its own,
to be thrown—heaved in fact
back into the unknown.

Haragei

(Japanese) Visceral, indirect, largely nonverbal communication.

The night she met him it snowed.
Turned the city silent
and white. He was air—
like seeing her own breath,
an open door, a glass of whisky,
one cube of ice.
He was the music she hummed, the neon
(that hummed too).
His jaw, a map—
her most certain path.
He shed winter with his coat,
held in his hands
all of the light,
all of it.

Hanyauku

(Rukwangali) The act of walking on tiptoes across warm sand.

Your roof is made of petals;
fallen, apple, pink.
In the wind, they swirl

pitch like longed-for rain.
Your bones, your sweet bones
lie hidden in the moss.

Your heart beats,
once for each grain of sand.
The sun nibbles

at your toes.
I collect the wind
that slips through the leaves

and in the shadows
spy the way
out.

Palatyi

(Bantu) A mythical monster that scratches at the door.

You cannot keep the moon
from your bed

the shadows from
your walls.

Cannot keep the birds
from singing all your dreams.

Rain becomes the body
you're yearning for.

The knock at your door,
begging *let me in*

to your lightning thoughts
your thunder heart.

Tingo

(Pascuense) The act of slowly taking all of the objects you desire from the house of a friend by gradually borrowing all of them.

You do not notice when I take the patterns
of leaves from your sill,

you still have the view of the garden
the wildflowers, the bees and the dragon

and damselflies.
Even dusk and dawn you hardly miss,

now that it is June and the days linger, stretch
both time and light into thin bands, into hope.

In July I take the porch, the stone pillars, the wooden floor
the table you and I both love,

the bottle and the glasses, the crickets and bullfrogs,
that one perennial moonlit toad—

it isn't until August, when you see the stray
scratching at my back door,

you notice how quiet your house is,
how empty the drawers.

Shibui

(Japanese) Beauty of aging.

When you go ten miles or a thousand
I go with you.

Carry your scent
in my hair.

Catch you,
on my tongue.

Walk with you until you are
my skin.

Mushin

*(Japanese) "Mind like water," "no-mind" or "empty mind,"
is a state where the mind is not preoccupied by any thought
or emotion.*

I sleep on my side, one arm thrown out.
Dream in color, dream
I am running, always running
Away. I'm a flee-er.
And a caster-about-er.
A paddler—water is my weakness
and anything made of it.
I type like I think, fluid and quick
like I love, like I drink—
kiss my wrist and you'll understand
why I can never find a pen
when I need one.

Salogok

(Eskimo–Aleut) Young black ice, a flexible sheet too thin to hold a man and weak enough for a seal to break through with their heads to breathe.

As a girl I was afraid of breaking him
the distance
from his shoulders
to the ground—me
with my marionette bones
my tangled strings.
He never understood
my terror, my fear
of the sky.
Just like I didn't understand clouds
and what kept me
from becoming one.
Holding my breath
lungs burning,
after he lowered me down, the air
the quick inhales,
like small pebbles in my mouth.
Wondering
how even in my sleep
(and when I dreamed of this)
I remember
to breathe.

Kintsukuroi

(Japanese) Golden repair. The belief that the breakage and repair becomes part of the history of an object, rather than something to disguise.

Like the lines of your hands
and the scars on my back
we wear our history

and when I look at you
all I can see
is your heart

the jagged lines;
each break, each bend
of gold.

Schilderwald

*(German) A street crowded with so many road signs that you
can become lost.*

A found poem based on t-shirts worn in Tokyo

Tell yourself
You're not going to like it

Please
Be kind

To show my
Knowledge
All the world

I had the dream
Again

Reckless
Waltz

Supreme effort

Bounce

Be your happiness
With the flower

What is the meaning
Of life

Hope
Springs
Eternal

The path
To the future

4 square & peace

Now, life is living you.

Tao

(Chinese) The way it goes (both noun and verb).

In a glass
what little remains, clings

The sound between the sounds
the silence

The drumming of my blood
in my veins

The way your eyelids
twitch when you dream

The thought
first waking

Barely ash
the smallest breeze

Word by word
and note by note

With the shadow
of a crow

Slip away
like silver like light.

Forelsket

(Norwegian) The euphoria experienced when you're first falling in love.

There are only the occasional lights
of the cars on the other shore
small, round and white, sometimes
red—although they are harder to see
from this distance. The lake
is black, as if all the colors
the clouds were at sunset,
spilled together.
Perhaps it is the sky's fault—
there is just so much of it.
Even the moon, now full and rising
is swallowed up
once it leaves the rim
of the water.

Mbuki-mvuki

(Bantu) To shuck off clothes in order to dance.

I have never been so cold;
cold for hours, cold for days. Cold so deep
my bones like concrete. My steps are careful. If I were to fall
I'd shatter, I'm certain. I am twenty-two. A northerner.
I am used to cold, but even the buses
aren't running, they won't start,
and so I walk. Walk the blocks,
the miles from the ESL class
I'm teaching, to my apartment
on Wrightwood, thinking about my students
all from somewhere else, somewhere
warmer, lush and green, and I am hoping
they understand how much they need to put on
coats, hats, mittens, boots, scarves
in Chicago, in January.
I know three of my students got my lesson today.
It was about opposites; putting things on
and taking things off.
They were sitting together, in a row, closer
to the back of the room than the front.
One is Indian, one Thai, one Japanese.
Raj raises his hand first, says *Teacher*
take off your hat.
Niran raises his hand next, says
Teacher take off your jacket.
Haruki, slowly raises his hand, smiles, then says
Teacher
Take off your shirt.

Kabelsalat

(German) Tangled up cables, literally "cable-salad."

I am working my way back
to a field from years ago—
one the sun had found
and the highway cut through—
quilted crops and a pony
stand near the ditch,
watching for you.
I've always loved the things
that don't need me; sky and rain,
broken-back barns,
the wilderness of you, you.
As hard as I try to untangle
the song from the dance,
the meaning from the words,
somehow I always end up here;
the sun to my left, the dust
from the road rising
in my rearview mirror.
Window rolled down
the scent of fire drifts in,
bullfrogs sing me home.

Ikigai

(Japanese) A reason to get up in the morning, a reason to live.

The sun has fallen behind the trees
and I can't see much difference
between blood and water;
both come and go,
both are a part of me.

There is nothing blacker
than a crow. Nothing quite like
the shadow one leaves
on me. Your shadow
is somewhere else tonight

casting long and lean—
streetlight, bar light, moonlight
any will do
for the love of you.
I will wait for the sun

to come, to kiss, then leave
the water. I will watch
its golden light,
fill all the blanks
and all the hollows.

Ondinnonk

(Iroquoian) The soul's innermost benevolent desires.

Save part of yourself
for me

The part the wind stirs; your branches,
your trembling leaves.

The part
That's hard to look back on.

The part the water
washes away, the fish chase.

The part the shadows find
turn cool and gray.

The part
only the stars see.

Save that
for me.

Dolilyts

(Ukranian) To lie with your face turned down to the ground.

To eat a peach
on this last day of summer
as night falls dense and dark. I sit
on the front porch, its light
burned out, I sit, peach in hand
its velvet skin warm like mine.
A small thank you, to bite
into flesh, soft and plenty, to feel
the stone on my teeth, hard
to let the juice run down my chin, not care, to let
the juice run down my neck, mingle
with the sweat and salt of me. To smell
its perfume, nibble
the stone clean, knowing
I can't make it last. Knowing
I can't make anything
beautiful
last.

Hozh'q

(Navajo) The beauty of life, as seen and created by a person.

The lake
so clear, so cold, so clean.
Not even you
can stop me
from diving in.
Open my eyes
see shafts of light
angle their way through.
Think of you
How you love me
Just like this.
My heart
a stone thrown,
your love
the ever-widening circles.

Stam

(Hebrew) For no reason, or because it's there.

Sometimes
it is your shadow
I crave
for it means
there is sun, bright and beautiful
and there is you,
making it.

Tsundoku

(Japanese) Buying books and not reading them; letting books
pile up on shelves or floors or nightstands.

My parents used to joke about making furniture out of them; in-
stead of being coffee table books, they could be the coffee table.
Ditto on nightstands, counters, roofs. When we were kids, my
brother and I, teased about always reading, built a wall. Right
through the middle of the neighborhood, protected ourselves with
fiction and with facts. I loved the encyclopedias best; the weight of
them, how my grandmother made me walk with one on my head
to practice being a lady. It wasn't until college that I built a grand
stairway out of them; their glossy blue jackets looked like marble
in the moonlight. I climbed it, to the top of the wall. Peering over, I
found you, on the other side, alone in your bed, asleep. That was
the first time you dreamed me. In your dream, you told me not to
jump. But to be patient. (We were young then, it would be years be-
fore we'd meet) and then this morning, I found you in my bedroom.
In your hands, *How to Rope and Tie a Steer*, a mug of coffee, a piece
of slightly burned toast. I took *The Sun Also Rises* from the wall,
made the first window into your heart.

Akihi

*(Hawaiian) Listening to directions then promptly walking off
and forgetting them.*

In the end she remembered her garden,
the ruby red spikes of rhubarb, pushing winter into spring,
the tight fists of peonies, the ants that accompanied them.

So she could sleep, her bedroom window thrown open;
the cool scent of earth, the soft sigh of wet branches,
the broken moon upon her face.

She is ash now, fragments of bone.
Her hair, her beauty, her soul
in flames set free.

I find her now
in the space between
the shadow and the light.

Biritululo

(Kiriwani) The act of comparing yams to settle a dispute.

In this one, love wins.
Dragonflies lead you
across the water,
their shadows fall
iridescent and blue.
Each memory
soft petals, the dust pollen
leaves on your skin.
And the bees—
in no hurry at all,
travel like the sun
through your day.
Leave night
to heat lightning
to love
to stories
to surprise endings.

Załatwiać

(Polish) Using acquaintances to accomplish things unofficially.

He isn't even using bait. We tried to find a worm or two, but all that was under the rocks was equally rocky soil. It is July in the Catskills and it hasn't rained in weeks. All the water around seems to sit in this pond, reflecting the traveling clouds, the sky's mood. My feet are in the water, my toes, small planets. In they come. One, then a half-dozen small olive-spotted fish. I do not know what kind they are. What fish are mountain fish? What fish find their way to a pond this small? The first never takes the hook. Swims up and by. But a second one darts from the pack and grabs hold. He catches five or six this way, in five or six minutes. It is too easy. We think it's my toenails painted silver that bring them in, but later even our shadows are enough.

Ya'aburnee

(Arabic) "You bury me"—the hope to die before another because it would be so difficult to live beyond that person.

Somewhere fireflies
light up a thicket.

Somewhere
a coyote howls.

You are a postcard, a rodeo
the lingering heat of summer on my skin.

I've never liked the sunset,
but I don't mind the quiet rising moon.

All I ask is that you bury me
in the dark

in the distance
between stars.

Tokka

(Finnish) A large herd of reindeer.

How many times can a shadow be trampled,
broken into bits of lost light

How much dust does it take to fill a belly,
Fill a heart

Till the blood
in your veins wants nothing

But to run,
join the pounding hooves.

Gestalten

(German) Little wholes that make up larger wholes.

After she left
you can close your eyes
and still see what once was;
the curve of the eaves and the shine
of the windows, the way sunlight traveled
the floor, crept its way
into bed with you.
Hear too
the creak of the steps
the ones she took
two at a time,
always
barefoot.

Poronkusema

(Finnish) The distance a reindeer could travel without stopping to urinate. A traditional "measure" of travel, not well-defined but allegedly 7.5 kilometers at maximum.

The sun never sets.
We are headed west
flying over Minot, North Dakota
then following the Alaskan coast
and its arc of islands. I try not to think about
time; how for the people on the ground below me
it is moving at a different rate, perhaps
more orderly, perhaps not.
Mine is measured in drinks
and movies. In trips to the bathroom.
We land in another day
in another city, in another country.
We will move
at the speed of a train,
then, the pace we walk.
In my head I picture the curve
of the islands, how Russia
looks no different from Korea,
from Alaska, from 40,000 feet.
Sometimes we need to see things
from a great distance
and sometimes, no distance at all.
No one here looks like me
but it is raining
and I am just another umbrella,
another set of legs, walking,
a mother holding the hand
of her tired son.

Naz

*(Urdu) The pride or confidence derived from knowing that
somebody holds you as the object of their affection and desire.*

Once upon a time there was a girl whose body was tattooed with
the shadows of leaves. Even her golden brown hair resembled the
bark of a tree. She became the patterns, the lacework of sun and
leaves and branches. She didn't mind. She loved trees. She loved that
she was part them. In the summer, she spent her time in the canopy,
lost in the branches. She lay there, waiting for the perfect angle of
the sun, to lay the tree's shadow in a perfect match to her skin.

Leaves have two sides. The one the sun sees (the moon and stars
too) and the other, the underside, what she saw, what she was. She
wasn't shiny or beautiful. She was pale-skinned and had veins you
could trace from her wrists to her heart. She imagined her bones
were branches; her thoughts, the wind. She knew that one day love
would take root. She'd stop in her tracks. She'd burst into blossom.
Be pinned to the earth.

Razbliuto

(Russian) The feeling a person has for someone he or she once loved but now does not.

A bed, white sheets—
wrap me in them
make my body disappear

The heat of me
just like the sun
warm upon your skin

I'll close my eyes.
You can leave yours open
if you want to

look into the sun
look into
all the forbidden things

watch the shadows play
upon the wall
watch them come, then go

trace the outline of what was my body
trace the outline
of what was my love.

Házisárkány

(Hungarian) "Home-dragon," an impatient or ill-natured spouse.

We keep the hall light on for them,
Read out loud their favorite stories,
Sing the sweetest lullabies, make up verses
Harmonize. We leave the windows curtainless
So the moonlight can find their scales.
We tell them how beautiful they are.
We thank them for their fire,
For their roar, for their sweeping tails.
The closet door, always left ajar.
Under the bed, dust, like tumbleweed,
we've spun into a soft pillow
for them to rest their heads.

Zeitgeist

(German) Spirit of the age or of the time.

I need a word
for the air around you—
a word that captures
the heat the spark the energy,
the way it moves and stills,
how it has the capacity to contain
music; familiar, new, never been heard before.
Not to mention memories of two-lane roads,
the windows rolled down the hum of tires,
the radio on—Wichita Lineman, Glen Campbell
now a part of it too, the dust
on the dashboard, the thin string of cellophane
with the gold line running through it
like the "no passing" line in the road.

As ancient as the men I come from.
As ancient as the grease and dirt and scars on their hands.
As ancient as love.

I need that word.

Friolero

(Spanish) A person who is especially sensitive to cold weather and temperature.

It is at the edges of night and morning
the dew, clear as tears, cannot hide
the cool, the shifting downward.

My skin, my summer love, is thinking
about everything I've taken off,
abandoned in dark spaces.

I don't want to think in layers.
Want to be toes, legs, arms,
bare shoulders.

I picture you
in a far-off land,
north and east of me.

You smell like woodsmoke
and deep spring-fed lakes,
mineral and mercurial. I picture you

in a world made of trees.
There are no highways that can bring me to you,
only stars, deer paths, moonlight.

Schnapsidee

(German) An ingenious plan one hatches while drunk.

We started documenting our plots in photo booths, in European
train stations. Then sleeping in cars, at the edge of soccer fields
(making it easier to get to the game).

There was Ouzo and hummus, the bar that was going to be named after
me. The walk back, after missing the last train. Walking the tracks
and singing to anyone who was still awake in Berlin.

Then, when we were in different countries,
late-night/early morning international phone calls
that lasted as long as our coins did.

You loved to wake me, let your voice and laughter spill
thousands of miles. Afterwards,
the world I was in seemed less than, sound minus sound.

Travel was always involved, changing time zones.
As was music
and a getaway car.

Rasa

(Sanskrit) The mood or sentiment evoked by a work of art.

My affair with Haruki Murakami
is three months old now. Becoming an everyday
kind of love. Even though I know he is a writer
I picture him working in a noodle shop.
His is solitary work; one of those narrow,
near-the-train-tracks shops in Tokyo.
His counters are stainless
steel and oh how they shine. His broth
the ideal golden blush. His onions, slivers,
his chives, thin blades. His edamame
the green of spring.
He builds each bowl of soba noodles
like he builds a sentence; noun upon noun
minced with verbs. Adjective you can smell, savor.
New, edible, landscapes to name.
And in each bowl a hint
of loneliness.
The kind a noodle shop man
Working alone
knows.

Funktionslust

(German) Pleasure taken in what one does best.

This is how we love. Wake before the sun. Bare feet, cold floor. No words, no thoughts until we fill our hands with something; saw or brush or metal strings, wood, the curve of a neck, sound, bread, the empty space. Catalog the birds that cross our paths. Catalog each glimmer, each flicker of light, each gray. Make a drink and drink it fast. Imagine ourselves wisps of smoke. Imagine ourselves unending. Find ourselves inside the music. We can't hide from our desires. Smash a berry between our fingers. Lick the juice, but leave the stain. Slowly undress in the moonlight. Slip between sheets cool as rain. Close our eyes, no thoughts, no words, just skin. Dream of this.

Friluftsliv

*(Norwegian) Literally "free air life," a way of life spent
exploring and appreciating nature.*

Yield to me your yellows, your falling
reds. Stand tall, limbs outstretched
against an ashen sky.
Let me see you, as the birds do
welcoming and deep-rooted. Let me
build in the crook
of your arm
a home.

Utepils

*(Norwegian) To enjoy a beer while sitting outdoors on a
really nice day.*

For the last day of July

There is something about this hour
that reminds me of you
the way time slows and even
the sky seems to want to sit down,
have a drink. Want to watch
the water bead, cling
to the glass, want to taste
what is left
in the melting ice.
Want to forget
everything I know
except the heat
of you.

When words no longer

I want a word for moonlight
trapped in an icicle,
for night cut clean
at the edge.

I want a word
that moves like you do
from room to room
leaving a trail of love.

I want a word yelled
from the screen door,
one that follows me
into the shade of the elms.

I want a word that lives
between leaves in the canopy,
that every sparrow sings,
that sounds just like your name.